THE PEACE WILL COME

(Through the Eyes of a Mother/Caregiver)

Karen Pettaway

WESTBOW
PRESS®
A DIVISION OF THOMAS NELSON
& ZONDERVAN

WestBow Press books may be ordered through booksellers or by contacting:

WestBow Press
A Division of Thomas Nelson & Zondervan
1663 Liberty Drive
Bloomington, IN 47403
www.westbowpress.com
1 (866) 928-1240

ISBN: 978-1-5127-9976-7 (sc)
ISBN: 978-1-9736-0869-1 (e)

Print information available on the last page.

WestBow Press rev. date: 10/24/2017

ACKNOWLEDGMENTS

To my husband: Dorial, for your loving and gentle spirit.

To my children: Marchina, Ronda and Dorial (DJ).

To my Parents: Clemia and Ceola Anderson, who went home to be with the LORD in January and August 2006. They showed and demonstrated their love for Jesus Christ and their children (Ret. Capt. US Navy Clemia Jr, James, Aaron, Crandell, Karen and Donna).

To my pastor for over twenty years: Dr. Aggie Pettaway-Hardy, who went home to be with the LORD in February 2015. Thank you for your spiritual teaching and wisdom.

CONTENTS

Subjects	Pages

DEDICATION

I dedicate this book to my husband *Dorial*. When we started on this journey with our son, we did not know what to expect or what steps to take. Having a child with a disability was a challenge to the both of us but we manage to take each day at a time. I thank you for standing strong with your family and making sure that we had everything that we needed as we travel this journey. I thank God for 30 wonderful years of marriage.

I dedicate this book to my daughters *Marchina and Ronda*. You were 10 and 5 years old when your brother was born. You were much too young to understand what was going on with him but the love that you both had for him out weight the things that may have puzzle you. Yes, I know it must have been hard seeing him go in and out the hospital at such a young age but God was there to comfort your hearts. Thank you for giving up so much just so he can have the best of everything. May God continue to bless the both of you.

I dedicate this book to my son *Dorial (DJ)*. Wow! What a joy it is having you as a son. This journey has been long, overwhelmed, hurtful, excited, and joyful. The answer will always and forever remain the same; I wouldn't trade it for nothing.

On this journey with you, I have learned so many things that I could have not learned anywhere else. The Lord Jesus place you in my life for a reason and he use YOU to show me how to be patience, loving, kindhearted and many, many more. You always had a smile no matter how sick you were and no matter how many times they had to stick you for blood work. You are amazing. As I watch you grow each year, it never was a dull moment with you. As being a child with Development Delay and Epilepsy, you manage to let nothing get in your way of being happy. On days that were not going well with me, you would look over at me and say, "What's wrong or make a funny gesture" where we both would start to laugh. At 21 years old, just look how far you have come in spite of all the hurdles you had to endure. You are Bless!!

DJ Favorite Bible Scripture
Proverbs 3:5-7

Trust in the LORD with all thine heart,
and lean not unto thine own understanding. In
all thy ways acknowledge him, and he shall direct thy paths.

Proverbs 3:5-7

INTRODUCTION

Life was good! The Lord had bless me with a wonderful husband and two beautiful daughters but there was still something missing, a son. The girls were now nine and four years old. It was the perfect time for them to have a brother.

That next year our son, DJ was born. It was wonderful. As the months went by, everything was peaceful. Suddenly around 2:00 a.m. we were awaking by DJ screaming to the top of his lungs.

THE JOURNEY

The journey was about to begin. I already plan what it would be like having a son. Mother knows best. Right. Wrong. God knows best. *Jeremiah 29:11 For I know the thoughts that I think toward you, saith the LORD, thoughts of peace, and not of evil, to give you and expected end.* I have always been a Christians but have not truly trusted the Lord. Well, my time has come.

The Peace Will Come.

DJ was 10 months old when we was awaking with the screaming and by the time we got him to the hospital his fever was high and when they finish all the tests, we was told that he had the Meningitis. Meningitis, what? How did he get that and where did he get it from. Well, as a mother, we never get used to hearing bad news concerning our children, and that was not what I was waiting to hear from the doctor. So, I position myself because I knew this was going to be a long, long journey.

He also was having seizures. As the months went by, he remained on the seizure medicine and I notice that he was not doing the basic skill according to his age that he should have been doing. I know that every child is not the same but he should have been doing something. At the age of 3 years old, he was enrolled in Early Invention to help strengthen his motor skills. He learn to sit up, walk with a walker and balance himself. By then I knew that this was a journey that I had to walk in faith because this was too big for me to handle.

The Peace Will Come.

I reach back and took out my spiritual road map (The Bible). Everything that you would ever need to know about life situations is in the Bible. *Philippians 4:7 And the peace of God, which passeth all understanding, shall keep your hearts and minds through Christ Jesus.* I really need some understand right about now. What happen and why this was happening? Was what I wanted to know? God had a plan and it was about to unfold.

The first day of Kindergarten was really scary for me. As DJ enters the school, I remember praying: Lord, I can't go with him and neither can I watch him, but you can. Will you send him someone that will be his friend and look out for him? Even though he was entering Kindergarten, a lot of the things that he should have been doing according to his age was not there. The teacher was wonderful and his classmates were great! They all looked after him as if he was their sibling. Peace was coming. My heart was feeling better and the Lord had answered my prayer. This was just the beginning and I know that there will be other hurdles to cross but we made it over this one with prayer and faith. We often forget what God word say, and we think we are left to walk this journey along but there is a peace. *John 14:27 Peace I leave with you, my peace I give you, not as the world giveth, give I unto you.* I needed that peace.

The elementary school years were great and everyone pitched in to lend a hand and make him feel a part of every activity that they had. He learn a lot and he could memorize things that some of the other children could not. That was just a start; he still had a long way to go. We found out that music was the key to help him learn. It's amazing how music can be used in so many ways and even help DJ learn his lesson. That's how he memorizes, but putting a beat to everything he does.

Another school year was getting ready to start and it was DJ middle school years.

During the summer just before school started, DJ was diagnosed with Developmental Delayed. This was another path that we had to deal with while we were just getting the handle on the issues that he was already facing. I thought we was on our way until we got this news. What, not another one. In spite of all this, **God is good!** Still on seizures medicine but he was doing well. Some of his motor skills were better but we still had a long way to go. A lot of his basic skills were not up to his age level but I had begun to reach out to other learning centers that would help strengthen them. The little things we take for granted means so much to a person with a disability. It's a struggle just for them to learn how to stay focus.

The first day of school was here. There were two of his classmates that had been with him from Kindergarten up until now. I was so grateful for that. By this, we are off to another good year. This journey is hard and if you haven't been through something like this, you don't know how it feels. All things happen for a reason good or bad and I was determine that something good was going to come out of this. So, I started looking here and there for things and places to help enhance his learning. The middle school was a challenge for children that did not have a disability so I knew that it was going to be a bit harder for him. DJ personality is easy and laid back. He loved to laugh and he is always happy. There is never a dull moment around him. Singing and dancing are his everyday thing and he did it every chance he got. I believe that's what help him get through his day. If he heard a beat of any kind, he would start dancing. All the kids in school knew that and it was a joy for them to see him so happy each day he enter the classroom. My spirit began to be at ease. During the school year, there were different activities held and I would go with DJ to them and it meant the world to him. We would get there early so we could get a seat where no one would have to step over him and leave a little early so the crowd would not gather all around him. I made adjustments. That was one thing that I had to constantly do if he was to survive. Did I always feel like making adjustments? No, it was not about me but him.

The Peace Will Come

THE ARRIVAL

Remember this verse, *Proverb 3:5-7 Trust in the LORD with all thine heart, and lean not unto thine own understanding. In all thy ways acknowledge him, and he shall direct thy paths.* This is the verse that took me all the way through DJ early years up unto now. With DJ being diagnosed with Meningitis and we also found out that he has a fluid blockage in the brain, this scripture became a part of my life. As a mother, we have big dreams for our children and when those dreams don't go the way we plan, we feel devastated.

During the summer, before entering his senior year the unthinkable happen. DJ started having more seizures so that mean he was put on another medication. The spirit of the Lord has a way of calmness and little did I know it at time but the LORD spirit had gripped my heart. I went into his senior year ready. *Psalm 63:3 Because thy lovingkindness is better than life, my lips shall praise thee.* We are to praise him in the good times and well as in the bad times. Easier said than done. Right. I know it. Trust me, this don't come over night. The big things that seniors look forward to such as: (senior trip, senior skip day, prom, graduation pictures and of course graduation) was not that important anymore to me. I had learned to accept whatever the LORD hand planned for him. Even though I looked forward to the senior year.

Well, DJ did take senior pictures, he attended prom with his sister and we took lots and lots of pictures on his prom night. Remember the two girls that I had mention earlier that was with him up until middle school. One of the girls helped assist him with walking up on the stage to get his diploma. *Isaiah 55:8 For my thoughts are not your thoughts, neither are your ways, my ways, saith the LORD.* I was thinking one way and the LORD thoughts about DJ were totally different from mines. See, just because things don't go the way we planned it doesn't mean it won't happen. I always had the support my family and friends and there were other people that I believe GOD sent my way. Before the peace would come there were some things that I had to do such as:

- Don't be afraid to let go and let GOD take full control
- Don't compare my son ability to another child ability
- Don't listen to negative talk
- Don't be afraid to trust (you can't do it alone)

When I realize this, things began to come together. It's not about what everyone else is saying, it's only about the plan that GOD has for you. So go ahead and let the tears flow because only then and ONLY THEN will you see the peace began to come.

I don't know what the future hold but I do know who holds the future and that's enough for me. This was a storm and I know that there will be many more on this life's journal. I am reminded of a scripture in the bible, *Mark 4:37-39 And there arose a great storm of wind, and the waves beat into the ship, so that it was now full. And he was in the hinder part of the ship, asleep on a pillow: and they awake him, and say unto him, Master, carest thou not that we perish? And he arose, and rebuked the wind, and said unto the sea, Peace, be still.* The LORD does care about us and even when we are going through storms in our life. There will be times when the storms will beat up on you and leave you with a feeling of isolation as if you are in it all by yourself. Have you ever notice that you can be around a group of people and still feel alone? Yes, it's possible. That's what was happening to the disciples. See, with some storms we get warnings and with some storms they just can pop up from anywhere. The storms that just pop up from anywhere leaves us afraid and helpless don't know what to do or where to run for safety. That's why it's good to have good Christian friends and even more better a prayer partner.

When I started on this journey, I must admit that I had three question that I needed answers to: What, When and Why? Just like other parents, we think it was something that we did for this to happen. Not so. *Psalm 139:14 I will praise thee; for I am fearfully and wonderfully made marvellous are they works, and that my soul knoweth right well.* In spite of everything DJ was fearfully and wonderfully made. So don't let the three W's take root in your heart any longer. The peace I need so desperately had finally come for this storm.

Whatever you are facing, don't go through it alone. There is help and people that are willing to give you a hand, if only to sit quietly with you. Whether you are a caregiver to a spouse, child, parent or grandparent, you can be surrounded in GOD's peace. Also, I found out that there were mothers that were just waiting for someone to open up the door and share their feeling (real feeling) about being a caregiver. I have learned so much on this journey that I probably would not have learned any other way. Patience is a big one for me. If

I am getting ready to go somewhere, I have never wanted to get dress and then wait. Well, I learn that in order for me to be somewhere on time, I would have to get dress first and then help DJ get dress because guess what, he don't like to get dress and wait. We have had some funny moments about that. There will be times when you will have to just laugh about it.

On this road with my son, it has not always been easily but I would not trade it for anything. Our family has learned to push and pull through all the bad as well as the good. I often tell people that the Lord Jesus is in control and I give it all to him. I recall this one incident that we had with a well-known learning center. We had taken DJ there for tutoring and fill out all the paperwork and paid the fee. Well, it was about two weeks when we went back for the first session and little did we know what was about to happen. They call us into a room and with these words, "we are returning your money because he will not be able to learn or keep up with the lesson". Right about now you know how those words hit me, just like a cement block hitting the ground. Like a mother, we hold things close to our heart. That was a hard, hard blow. The drive was a long, quiet drive back home, even some tears was shed. Sometimes people in general don't realize that the words they say cut just like a knife and yet they don't think twice when they say them. We made it back home and I didn't tell anyone what was said to me.

Walking in hurt, I began to ask the Lord Jesus what to do. He gave me a plan. I started a parent support group. I did not want any parent to be hurt the way I did. At the first meeting, there was a mother of a little girl that was just waiting on someone to hear her story. It was not easy starting this support group but I just could not sit back and let a parent experience some of the things that I had experience. I had attended some support groups and there were some good ones and some bad ones but nevertheless I had to at least try it. By attending them I wanted to see how they operated and what was going on inside of the group. I wanted the support group that I started to be that whoever came would feel comfortable enough to open up and tell their true feeling. So, it had to start with me. The Lord Jesus had me in a realm that I could really tell how I felt.

As I began to tell how I felt, the peace just over shadow me. Too many families go through this alone and when that happens there is a break down in the home. We have to get to a place where even in our busy schedule, we stop and be REAL. It's hard but it gets better over time. This was something that we had to really adjust to. We could not just jump up and go when we got ready because DJ was one that you could not hurry. Before DJ would even leave his room, everything had to be lined up straight or put away. His toys, shoes, paper, books or whatever he was doing, it had to be put in order. That was something I notice when he was little just before we got ready to leave the house. It's still a big one for him today. Many people go and leave everything the way it is until they get back home and stuff is all over the floors and dishes in the sink. I had to learn to get up him up earlier and give him the time he needed to put things away before we left home. Whenever I woke up late and push for time, I knew what I was in for. Learning the little things they like or dislike will make the day go by easier.

The teenage years were a challenge also for me. It's like I had to find things to keep him busy. He loves music and still does, so we made sure that he had plenty of CD's and DVD's to play and watch. We would hear him from the other room singing and dancing. We learn to give him his space.   He learn to use the computer because they use them at school. At home he was able to use the computer and find simple programs that were on his level of understanding. God is good!

Two years before DJ finish high school, the company I work for down sized and I was let go. What a blessing in disguise. At first, I did not look at it that way but that allowed me the freedom to become more involved in finding activities for him. A friend of mine told me about the Miracle League baseball program that was available in my area. So, I signed him up for that. I remember when I got the email with the coach name, players and team he would be playing on in the spring. Even though I was happy, fear began in set in because he has never even held a bat and you talking about playing ball. I call the coach and began to give him a long list of things that DJ could not do and he said," just bring him". Well, that Saturday morning we were on our way. When we got there and I saw the mothers, fathers and sibling of the ones that was disable and how much fun they were having, I knew right then that this would be something for us to do every year. We as a family looked forward to this and we had fun. The coaches and buddies were amazing. It's been three years and DJ is still playing ball. Go DJ!!

Again, I found a recreation center where I enroll him and the first day he attended the class, fear tried to grip my heart. I began to pray and ask the Lord Jesus to take care of him and watch over him.

I left him for 4 hours and counted each second, minute and hour until I went to pick him up. When I arrived there and went in to get him, he was sitting at a table surrounded by young people talking and laughing. They were talking about how he had been singing and dancing. Yes, he loves to perform.

The peace from our Lord Jesus has come so many times to me on this journey. Even at times when I felt alone or with a room full of people, the peace was there. See, it like this, we never adjust to things that we can't change because we love to be in charge. We can't fix our children, only God can. We can't fix a disability, only God can.

Learn all that you can about your child. Ask God for wisdom because you will need it.

> *If any of you lack wisdom, let him ask of God, that giveth*
> *to all men liberally, and upbraideth not;*
> *and it shall be given him,*
> **James 1:5**

I learn to read him (so to speak) just like I would read a book. I had to know and learn how to get him to do things a little different. Out of the ordinary, DJ development skills are low but he learn by watching and seeing. We often talk about how he find whatever he want to watch on the TV, and how he can find the program on the computer without asking someone to do it for him. He can identify one word and find what he need. Learning to be creative has helped him so much.

As a mother and a caregiver to my son, I often wonder at the end of the day how I made it through that day. I start my day by getting up earlier while everyone is sleep and get my time in with worship and reading my bible. Because once the day starts, it's rolling all day. Time alone is very important to a caregiver because we give, and give so much of ourselves. We cannot live in isolation and we cannot live with regrets.

- Don't regret that you didn't get it right the first time you tried to understand how they function.
- Don't regret if you have to leave them for a few hours with someone else.
- Don't regret taking time for yourself.

I must say that all the above was me. Let me be real. The last one should be first on the list because if I get frustrated or get burn out, how will I be able to care for him. So I learn to take some time and just breathe.

My husband, daughters and family member would watch him from time to time if I needed to run an errand. There were also times when I would ride him with me just so he wouldn't have to stay at home. Keeping DJ close by my side was what I did but as time went by I could hear the Lord saying, "trust me with him", and that's when I start realizing the peace. I was only hurting myself. In the midst of trusting the Lord Jesus with him, I started surrounding my daily activities with positives thoughts. Focusing on the things that DJ could do and not so much on what he could not do. This scripture were very helpful.

> *Wait on the Lord; be of good courage, and he*
> *Shall strengthen thine heart: wait, I say on the*
> *Lord.*
> **Psalm 27:14**

FRIENDSHIP

When we think of making friends, sometimes it's hard to start the conversation. It's easy for children but we all need friends. As a mother, I use to think that I did not have time for friends and especially not now. But was I so wrong. The Lord will send people our way and at the right time. Not all will remain with you but there are those that will stay. I found out that the ones that stay they are your true friends. Also, I learn that a friend does not have to be with you all the time but when you need them they are there no matter what.

Beautiful friendships can be formed out of a caregiver's journey. I have two mothers and a prayer partner that I can call on at any time. We try to get together with our kids and just hang out sometime. They need that just as much as we do. You will gains friends along the way and you will lose friends along the way on this journey. But remember, a true friend will always be there. *Proverbs 18:24 A man that hath friends must shew himself friendly; and there is a friend that sticketh closer than a brother.*

Don't close yourself out. The world needs caregivers: mothers, fathers, grandparents, aunts, and uncles. Be a friend and let's show them just how important it is to remain friends in the thick and thin of being caregivers. Within the parent support group, I look for ways to bring the families out and I recall when I had a Valentine/Mardi Gras Ball, it was amazing to see the families (including the person with the disability) attend the ball. Just to see the smiles on their faces was priceless. I made it known that if the person with the disability could attend please bring them out. The ball was two hours and all of them was able to stay for the entire ball and was given goodie bags when they left. DJ had a good time.

Parents have lots of stories to share about the progress of their child and who would accept it better that someone who knows how you feel, a true friend. Choose them wisely.

Here are some scripture that I found to be helpful:

*The LORD bless thee, and keep thee: the
LORD make his face shine upon thee and give
thee peace*
Numbers 14:24-25

*Thou wilt keep him in perfect peace, whose
mind is stayed on thee; because
he trusteth in thee*
Isaiah 26:3

*GOD is our refuge and strength, a
very present help in trouble*
Psalm 46:1

*Be still, and know that I am GOD: I will
be exalted among the heathen, I will
be exalted in the earth*
Psalm 46:10

FROM MY HEART
TO YOURS

A mother holds so many things in her heart. She guards her heart from being broken over and over again and when something comes along that she do not understand it takes a toll on her. When DJ was growing up, I would get so upset about the things that were happening and it seemed like no one understood me. I wanted to shield him from the world and keep him close to me. I would often say where are you Lord? Do you see what I am going through and do you care? Yes, my husband and children was there but I wanted to hear from the Lord. As I began to turn loose and give up, that's when the peace start coming.

From my heart to your heart, let go and start taking one step at a time, step by step. The steps are hard at first just like a weight wrap around your ankle but keep on stepping. Raising a child with a disability is not easy and many, many times it can be a challenge but just know that you can do it and you are not in this along.

DJ is now 21 years old and what a challenge I have been through with him. We both have learned from each other. I must say that there are still moments where I would like to shield him from the world. His personality is easy going, he loves to have fun and always smiling and that tells me that, he okay. In the last two years, he has been in and out the hospital so many times that I sit an amaze how he can be at peace no matter how many times they come to get blood or x-rays.

My heart hurts sometimes just seeing all that he goes through. The Lord is good. I am reminded of this scripture:

Because thy lovingkindness is better than life,
my lips shall praise thee,
Psalm 63:3

From my heart to your heart, start thanking the Lord for whatever in going on and I promise you, your heart will start to feel better. Things began to happen in my life and I start looking at the situation differently. I grew in the spirit, so to speak. I started to trust the Lord and then start being honest with myself. Honest about how I really felt. It takes a strong person to admit that they need help. We as mothers try to keep everything together and make sure that the family has everything they need but wait a minute, what about me (mother). I know the whole family pitch in together and that how it supposed to be but just in case they are all busy, we put off what we have plan and take care of it. We (mothers) catch a nap here and there, read a little, and if we are not careful we will get burned out. Then that's when everything gets on our nerves. I have been there. DJ is truly a blessing from the Lord and he keeps us laughing but I notice that there are times when he needs some peace and quiet. He needs his space to. So when I see that, I step back and let him have his time. Just look how it worked out for the both of us.

The Peace is here

As a caregiver to you child, always remember all they need is LOVE. I would like to share this scripture with you. When you feel that you cannot go any further remember this:

The Lord is my rock, and my fortress, and my deliverer, my God,
my strength, in whom I will trust; my buckler, and
the horn of my salvation, and my high tower.

Psalm 18:2

BIOGRAPHY

Karen Pettaway, is a wife, mother of three and a full time caregiver to her son. She is the president of a non-profit organization for young adults with disabilities. Karen and her husband Dorial have been married for 30 years.

Printed in the United States
by Baker & Taylor Publisher Services